AF885552

IN THE SENATE OF THE UNITED STATES
Sitting as a Court of Impeachment

In re **IMPEACHMENT OF** **PRESIDENT DONALD J. TRUMP**

REPLY MEMORANDUM OF THE UNITED STATES HOUSE OF REPRESENTATIVES IN THE IMPEACHMENT TRIAL OF PRESIDENT DONALD J. TRUMP

United States House of Representatives

Jamie Raskin
Diana DeGette
David Cicilline
Joaquin Castro
Eric Swalwell
Ted Lieu
Stacey Plaskett
Madeleine Dean
Joe Neguse

U.S. House of Representatives Managers

TABLE OF CONTENTS

INTRODUCTION

President Trump's pre-trial brief confirms that he has no good defense of his incitement of an insurrection against the Nation he swore an oath to protect. Instead, he tries to shift the blame onto his supporters, and he invokes a set of flawed legal theories that would allow Presidents to incite violence and overturn the democratic process without fear of consequences. His brief—in which he refuses to accept responsibility for his actions—highlights the danger he continues to pose to the Nation he betrayed. To send a clear message to the Nation and to all future Presidents that efforts to undermine our democracy through violence will not be tolerated, the Senate should convict President Trump and disqualify him from ever holding office again.

President Trump's constitutional offense is a matter of public record that cannot be seriously disputed. After spending months propagating the lie that the 2020 election had been stolen from him, President Trump summoned his supporters to a rally in Washington on January 6. He seized on that date—when Congress and the Vice President were to hold a Joint Session to count the Electoral College votes—as his last chance to overturn the election and install himself in the White House for a second term against the will of the majority of Americans.

Against this backdrop, President Trump addressed a crowd that he knew was armed and primed for violence. He falsely raged to the crowd that the Joint Session was the culmination of a treasonous plot to destroy America. He exhorted his supporters to "fight like hell [or] you're not going to have a country anymore." And he urged the mob to march to the Capitol, telling them that "[y]ou'll never take back our country with weakness." He thus lit the match of insurrection and threw it into the powder keg he had spent months creating. President Trump now studiously ignores all that preceded his speech and provided meaning and context to his statements, asking the Senate to do the same and focus only on a handful of his remarks in isolation.

There can be no doubt that President Trump is singularly responsible for inciting the violent insurrection that followed his speech. The mob he incited stormed the Capitol, bludgeoned the police with weapons, deployed chemical irritants, hunted Vice President Pence and Speaker Pelosi for their alleged "treason," and left threatening messages for Members of Congress—all the while proclaiming proudly that they were doing President Trump's bidding. By the end of the day, a police officer and four others were dead, dozens more were injured, and our Nation's Capitol was desecrated. As a direct result of President Trump's actions, the seat of our democracy has been transformed into a military camp. That is President Trump's legacy to the Nation.

Nor can there be any doubt that President Trump failed to act decisively to stop the violence as soon as it began. Instead, President Trump was "delighted" that the insurrection was delaying the counting of the Electoral College votes. In an astonishing act of further incitement and betrayal, President Trump denounced his own Vice President on Twitter *at the very time* the mob hunted him through the halls of the Capitol. When President Trump finally issued a statement after hours of delay, he blamed Congress for the attack on itself, and told the insurrectionists, "you're very special," and "we love you." Since then, he has described his conduct as "totally appropriate."

There can be no doubt that these facts amount to an impeachable offense. President Trump incited the insurrection while seeking to cheat in an election and remain in office for a second term against the will of America's voters. The Framers of our Constitution designed the impeachment power to protect against a President who would subvert our democracy to keep himself in power.

And the drafters of the Fourteenth Amendment further confirmed that an official who participates in an insurrection must be disqualified from future officeholding.[1] President Trump's conduct on January 6 was the paradigm of an impeachable offense.

Because President Trump's guilt is obvious, he seeks to evade responsibility for inciting the January 6 insurrection by arguing that the Senate lacks jurisdiction to convict officials after they leave office. This discredited argument has been rejected by scholars across the political spectrum, including many of the Nation's leading conservative constitutional lawyers, one of whom recently took to the pages of the Wall Street Journal to urge the Senate to accept jurisdiction over this trial. This argument has also been rejected by the very scholars on which President Trump principally relies, several of whom have taken *exactly the opposite position* as the position President Trump incorrectly ascribes to them in his trial memorandum. President Trump's jurisdictional argument is both wrong as a matter of constitutional law and dangerous as a matter of Senate practice. It would leave the Senate powerless to hold Presidents accountable for misconduct committed near the end of their terms. It would also create an obvious loophole in the Senate's disqualification power by allowing officials to resign immediately before their Senate trial. And it would encourage Presidents to commit abuses precisely when those abuses pose the greatest threat to our democracy—at election time. The Senate must reject this effort to eviscerate its impeachment power, just as it has rejected similar arguments in impeachments dating back more than 200 years.

President Trump's other defenses are equally weak. The First Amendment protects our democratic system—but it does not protect a President who incites his supporters to imperil that

---

[1] U.S. Const. amend. XIV, § 3.

system through violence. In the words of the Nation's leading First Amendment scholars, the argument that the First Amendment prevents the Senate from convicting the President is "legally frivolous."[2] Accepting President Trump's argument would mean that Congress could not impeach a President who burned an American flag on national television, or who spoke at a Ku Klux Klan rally in a white hood, or who wore a swastika while leading a march through a Jewish neighborhood—all of which is expression protected by the First Amendment but would obviously be grounds for impeachment. The First Amendment does not immunize President Trump from impeachment or limit the Senate's power to protect the Nation from an unfit leader. And even assuming the First Amendment applied, it would certainly not protect President Trump's speech on January 6, which incited lawless action.

President Trump's other purported defenses also fail. President Trump received all the process he was due. The House moved urgently to impeach him because he remained a danger after January 6. And President Trump's *trial* will occur in the Senate, which has provided for extensive pretrial briefing and an opportunity for him to present evidence before the Senate determines whether to convict. President Trump is also wrong to argue that he can only be impeached for a criminal violation. This argument has no support in history or precedent—and, once again, even the scholar on whom he relies has rejected it. Finally, President Trump's argument that the article of impeachment charges "multiple alleged wrongs" is simply false: the article charges a single course of impeachable conduct for inciting an insurrection.

* * *

[2] *Constitutional Law Scholars on President Trump's First Amendment Defense* at 1-2 (Feb. 5, 2021).

The question whether President Trump should be convicted and disqualified is not close. As the House Republican Conference Chair recognized, "There has never been a greater betrayal by a President of the United States of his office and his oath to the Constitution."[3] To deter future Presidents from attempting to subvert our Nation's elections, and to ensure that President Trump never again has an opportunity to endanger our democracy, the Senate should convict him and disqualify him from holding "any Office of honor, Trust or Profit under the United States."[4]

ARGUMENT

PRESIDENT TRUMP'S ATTEMPTED DEFENSES FAIL

Unable to defend his misconduct on January 6, President Trump devotes the majority of his brief to attempting to shift the blame to others, arguing that the Senate should not hold a trial at all, and trying to cloak his betrayal of the Nation in the First Amendment. All of his defenses fail.

A. President Trump Cannot Reasonably Deny Responsibility For Inciting The Insurrection

President Trump asserts that the insurrectionists stormed the Capitol "of their own accord and for their own reasons."[5] That argument defies belief. The factual record, as discussed in detail in our opening brief, demonstrates President Trump's singular responsibility for inciting the attack on the Capitol. That he does not like being held responsible by Congress does not allow him to rewrite history.

Before January 6, President Trump had tried and failed to overturn the election through every conceivable means at his disposal—flawed judicial challenges, threats against state officials,

[3] Liz Cheney, *I Will Vote To Impeach The President* (Jan. 12, 2021).
[4] U.S. Const., Art. I, § 3, cl. 7.
[5] Opp. at 9.

efforts to change state law, and even attempts to enlist his Attorney General to find proof of widespread fraud—all while he falsely insisted to his supporters that the election had been stolen from him.[6] After these methods failed, President Trump identified the Joint Session's electoral vote count as his final chance to retain his grip on the Presidency. He therefore planned a rally for the morning of January 6, just hours before Congress and the Vice President were to convene to affirm President Biden's election victory. He announced that he would personally appear at the rally, which he promoted constantly. The event "will be wild!"[7] he promised; a "historic day"[8] to "StopTheSteal!"[9]

By the morning of the rally, President Trump knew that many of his supporters, agitated by his barrage of lies about a stolen election, were prone to violence. An earlier pro-Trump rally in Washington, D.C. had ended in brawls, vandalism directed against churches, and numerous assaults on police officers.[10] One GOP election official even warned President Trump that his rhetoric

---

[6] William Cummings et al., *By the Numbers: President Donald Trump's Failed Efforts to Overturn the Election*, USA Today (Jan. 6, 2021); Michael Balsamo, *Disputing Trump, Barr Says No Widespread Election Fraud*, Associated Press (Dec. 1, 2020); Jesse Byrnes, *Barr Told Trump that Theories About Stolen Election Were "Bulls---": Report*, The Hill (Jan. 18, 2021); Amy Gardner & Paulina Firozi, *Here's the Full Transcript and Audio of the Call Between Trump and Raffensperger*, Wash. Post (Jan. 5, 2021); Maggie Haberman et al., *Trump Targets Michigan in His Ploy to Subvert the Election*, N.Y. Times (Nov. 19, 2020); Amy Gardner et al., *Trump Asks Pennsylvania House Speaker for Help Overturning Election Results, Personally Intervening in a Third State*, Wash. Post (Dec. 8, 2020); Ryan Randazzo et al., *Arizona Legislature 'Cannot and Will Not' Overturn Election, Republican House Speaker Says*, Arizona Republic (Dec. 4, 2020).

[7] Donald J. Trump (@realDonaldTrump), Twitter (Dec. 19, 2020, 1:42 AM).

[8] Donald J. Trump (@realDonaldTrump), Twitter (Jan. 3, 2021, 10:27 AM).

[9] Donald J. Trump (@realDonaldTrump), Twitter (Jan. 1, 2021, 2:53 PM).

[10] Peter Hermann & Keith Alexander, *Proud Boys Leader Barred From District By Judge Following His Arrest*, Wash. Post (Jan. 5, 2021); Jason Slotkin et al., *4 Stabbed, 33 Arrested After Trump Supporters, Counterprotesters Clash in D.C.*, NPR (Dec. 12, 2020); NBC Washington Staff, *4 Stabbed, 33 Arrested as Trump Supporters, Counterprotesters Clash in Downtown DC*, NBC Washington (Dec. 12, 2020).

would cause someone "to get killed."[11] When he stood at the podium before thousands of his supporters, President Trump knew that they were armed and that they were angry.

President Trump then whipped his followers into a frenzy. He launched into an impassioned attack on a "stolen election"[12]—falsely telling the crowd that Congress's actions at the Joint Session would be the culmination of a vast conspiracy to destroy the country. And President Trump made clear what he wanted them to do: go to the Capitol and "fight like hell." He told the crowd to march to the Capitol, even falsely pledging to join them on the march. He told them that "if you don't fight like hell you're not going to have a country anymore."[13] He added: "you'll never take back our country with weakness."[14]

President Trump cannot credibly claim that he is not responsible for what followed. As Leader McConnell accurately put it, "[t]he mob was fed lies" and "provoked by the president."[15] The insurrectionists themselves made clear that they understood that they were following President Trump's commands—they proudly said so in videos taken as they ransacked the Capitol, in statements to reporters after the riot, and in court when attempting to explain their heinous actions.[16] The many American flags wielded by attackers demonstrated that they believed they were performing a patriotic act in the service of their President. The rioters attacked the Capitol because

---

[11] Stephen Fowler, *'Someone's Going To Get Killed': Ga. Official Blasts GOP Silence On Election Threats*, NPR (Dec. 1, 2020).

[12] Donald J. Trump (@realDonaldTrump), Twitter (Nov. 8, 2020, 9:17 AM).

[13] *Watch LIVE: Save America March at The Ellipse featuring President @realDonaldTrump*, RSBN TV (Jan. 6, 2021); *Donald Trump Speech "Save America" Rally Transcript January 6*, Rev (Jan. 6, 2021).

[14] *Id.*

[15] Mike DeBonis & Paul Kane, *Uncertainty Reigns in Senate as Schumer Pushes Fast Agenda and McConnell Calls Out Trump*, Wash. Post (Jan. 19, 2021).

[16] Zoe Tillman, *Trump Supporters' Own Explanations For Assaulting The Capitol Are Undercutting His Impeachment Defense*, BuzzFeed News (Feb. 2, 2021); House Trial Mem. at 27-28.

President Trump plied them with false assertions that Congress and the Vice President were in the process of stealing their democracy.

President Trump argues that he "did not direct anyone to commit lawless actions,"[17] but as the crowd well knew, he had been urging Vice President Pence to do just that: by unilaterally and unconstitutionally overturning the election results at the Joint Session. President Trump's unsuccessful attempt to pressure Vice President Pence into acting unlawfully surely inspired the mob to believe that it needed to attack the Capitol—and to hunt down the Vice President himself when he refused.

If, as President Trump suggests, the mob "completely misunderstood him,"[18] and if he disapproved of the violence perpetrated by those who purported to act in his name, he could have acted swiftly to set them straight. But he refused. Instead, he was "delighted" by the riot at the Capitol because he believed it increased his chances of overturning the election. He even tweeted an attack on his own Vice President while the riot was underway.[19] Only after receiving public and private entreaties did he issue a pair of lukewarm tweets asking his supporters to "[s]tay peaceful" even as they committed horrific violence.[20] Finally, *three hours* after the siege began, he released a scripted video telling insurrectionists "We love you, you're very special. … I know how you feel."[21] Even then, he insisted that the election was "stolen from us"[22]—the same lie that had incited his

[17] Opp. at 11.
[18] Opp. at 11.
[19] Donald J. Trump (@realDonaldTrump), Twitter (Jan. 6, 2021, 2:24 PM).
[20] Donald J. Trump (@realDonaldTrump), Twitter (Jan. 6, 2021, 2:38 PM).
[21] Donald J. Trump (@realDonaldTrump), Twitter (Jan. 6, 2021, 4:17 PM); *President Trump Video Statement on Capitol Protestors*, C-SPAN (Jan. 6, 2021).
[22] *Id.*

supporters to commit violence in the first place. And in the evening, after the insurrection was finally put down, he blamed it on Congress: "These are the things and events that happen when a sacred landslide election victory is so unceremoniously & viciously stripped away from great patriots who have been badly & unfairly treated for so long."[23] President Trump barely attempts to justify his abject failure to stop the riot after it began, and confines his entire discussion of the point to a convoluted footnote that hardly offers any response or explanation at all.[24]

President Trump only *increases* his own responsibility by pointing to indications that some of the attackers planned the insurrection "*several days* in advance of the rally."[25] That fact underscores that President Trump knew exactly what he was doing in his campaign to overturn the election. Any plans hatched in advance were intended to support President Trump, who had inflamed his followers and invited them to converge in Washington, D.C., on January 6 to "StoptheSteal." His continued insistence that he was the rightful winner of the election was the oxygen that enabled their plans to flourish. And his incendiary remarks at the rally itself, delivered despite warnings that the crowd was poised and prepared for violence at his instigation, were the match that detonated everything. Had he accepted the verdict of the Electoral College—like *every* presidential candidate before him—there would have been no plans, no rally, no calls to "fight," and no insurrection.

Finally, President Trump does not help his case by arguing that his January 6 speech was intended to encourage his supporters to press for "election security generally."[26] To call this argument implausible would be an act of charity. The rally, set for the day when Congress was to

---

[23] Donald J. Trump (@realDonaldTrump), Twitter (Jan. 6, 2021, 6:01 PM).
[24] Opp. at 3 n.8.
[25] Opp. at 8.
[26] Opp. at 52.

count the electoral votes, was the culmination of President Trump's months-long campaign to overturn the results of a *specific* election he lost. In his speech, President Trump did not direct his supporters to go home and lobby their state legislatures, but instead directed them to march to the Capitol and fight. President Trump's speech did not promote election security—it exhorted a mob to attack Congress in order to overturn a free and fair election.

B. The Senate Has Jurisdiction To Try This Impeachment

President Trump is wrong to cast doubt on the Senate's jurisdiction over this trial. Scholars from across the political spectrum, including renowned conservative constitutional scholars, have recognized that the Constitution empowers the Senate to convict and disqualify officials who commit misconduct late in their terms and therefore can realistically only be tried after leaving office. We thus explained in our opening brief that there is no "January Exception."

As the former Reagan Administration official Chuck Cooper recently wrote in the Wall Street Journal, scholarship regarding the Senate's jurisdiction "has matured substantially" since this body voted on that question.[27] This scholarship "has exposed the serious weakness" in President Trump's claim that the Senate lacks jurisdiction.[28] For the reasons given by Cooper and others, Senators who previously voted to reject jurisdiction over this trial might wish to "reconsider their view and judge the former president's misconduct on the merits."[29]

Constitutional Text: President Trump's brief glaringly fails to address the constitutional text that establishes the Senate's jurisdiction over this trial. The language of the Constitution gives the

---

[27] Chuck Cooper, *The Constitution Doesn't Bar Trump's Impeachment Trial*, Wall Street Journal (Feb. 7, 2021).
[28] *Id.*
[29] *Id.*

Senate "the sole Power to try all Impeachments"[30]—not just impeachments involving sitting officials. As noted by Michael McConnell, a prominent scholar and former court of appeals judge appointed by President George W. Bush, the key word in the Constitutional text is "all."[31] "This clause contains no reservation or limitation" and it does not "say the Senate has power to try impeachments against sitting officers."[32] The constitutional text thus "makes clear that the Senate has power to try th[is] impeachment."[33]

The Senate's jurisdiction in this case is especially clear given that the House undisputedly had jurisdiction to impeach President Trump while he was still President. Regardless of whether the *House* would have the authority to commence an impeachment proceeding against an official after he left office, the *Senate* plainly has authority to try the impeachment of an official like President Trump who was still in office when he was impeached. Indeed, President Trump's attorneys attempt to support their jurisdictional argument by citing scholars who have said exactly the opposite of what President Trump ascribes to them; they have confirmed that the Senate possesses jurisdiction in these circumstances. For example, one article that President Trump relies on[34] concludes: "as long as an officer served in office at the time formal impeachment proceedings started, then the House and Senate retain jurisdiction to continue the process because the officer was 'in office' at the

[30] U.S. Const., Art. I, § 3, cl. 6.

[31] Eugene Volokh, *Impeaching Officials While They're in Office, but Trying Them After They Leave*, The Volokh Conspiracy (Jan. 28, 2021) (quoting Prof. Michael McConnell).

[32] *Id.*

[33] *Id.*

[34] Opp. at 19, 31, 36.

commencement of the proceedings."[35] Another scholar that President Trump repeatedly cites[36] recently opined: "Trump's defenders will surely contend that a president cannot be tried by the Senate after he has left office. They are wrong."[37] President Trump's brief's serious distortion of these scholars' views is deeply troubling.

Rather than tackle the Senate's unqualified power to try *all* impeachments or accurately represent the scholarship on this question, President Trump instead mistakenly invokes other constitutional provisions that he claims limit the Senate's power by implication. He cites the provision of Article I stating that "Judgment in Cases of Impeachment shall not extend further than to removal from Office, and disqualification to hold and enjoy any Office of honor, Trust or Profit under the United States."[38] This provision means that the Senate may not impose judgments that "extend further" than (1) removal of the accused if he remains in office, and (2) disqualification of the accused regardless of whether he remains in office. But nothing in this provision confines the Senate's disqualification power to cases involving sitting officials.

President Trump argues that because only sitting officials are subject to the removal remedy, then *only* sitting officials should be subject to the separate disqualification remedy.[39] But this argument attempts to add a word to the Constitutional text—"only"—that the Framers omitted. It also defies logic. If a law sets out two possible penalties and one of them becomes unavailable, that

---

[35] Harold J. Krent, *Can President Trump Be Impeached As Mr. Trump? Exploring the Temporal Dimension of Impeachments*, 95 Chi.-Kent L. Rev. 537, 548 (2021) (emphasis added).

[36] Opp. at 17, 20-21.

[37] Brian C. Kalt & Frank Bowman, *Congress Can Impeach Trump Now and Convict Him When He's Gone*, Wash. Post (Jan. 11, 2021). Professor Kalt has noted that, in several places, President Trump's brief contains "multiple . . . flat-out misrepresentations" of his scholarship. Brian Kalt (@ProfBrianKalt), Twitter (Feb. 8, 2021, 11:57 AM).

[38] U.S. Const., Art. I, § 3, cl. 7.

[39] Opp. at 30.

does not mean that the offender is exempt from the penalty that remains. Consider the example of a "con man" convicted under a statute that provides for both mandatory refund of the proceeds of his crime as well as a prison term. Even if the "con man" spends all the proceeds of his crime before his trial, thus making the refund penalty unavailable, he is obviously still subject to the penalty of imprisonment.[40]

President Trump also cites the provision of Article II stating that "The President, Vice President and all civil Officers of the United States, shall be removed from Office" upon impeachment and conviction.[41] This provision means that sitting officials who are impeached and convicted must be removed from office. But, as Cooper explains, this provision "cuts *against*" the theory that the Senate lacks jurisdiction over former officials.[42] Instead, this provision "simply establishes what is known in criminal law as a 'mandatory minimum' punishment: If an incumbent officeholder is convicted by a two-thirds vote of the Senate, he is removed from office as a matter of law."[43] It does not exempt former officials, and it certainly does not support the illogical leap that former officials are altogether immune from the Senate's power to try all impeachments.

The Constitution itself makes clear that the category of officials who can be tried in the Senate is broader than the category of "civil officers" who must be removed from office upon conviction. When the Constitution refers to the full category of individuals who can be tried by the Senate, it refers to "persons" and "parties"[44]—a broader category than the sitting "civil officers"

---

[40] *See* Frank O. Bowman, III, *The Constitutionality of Trying a Former President Impeached While in Office*, Lawfare (Feb. 3, 2021).

[41] Opp. at 18; U.S. Const., Art. II, § 4.

[42] Chuck Cooper, *The Constitution Doesn't Bar Trump's Impeachment Trial*, Wall Street Journal (Feb. 7, 2021).

[43] *Id.*

[44] U.S. Const., Art. I, § 3, cl. 6, 7.

subject to mandatory removal. President Trump does not even attempt to answer this point. Notably, President Trump filed a lengthy brief, but failed to engage with key jurisdictional arguments grounded in the Constitution's actual text.

President Trump next cites the provision stating that "When the President of the United States is tried, the Chief Justice shall preside."[45] This provision requires the Chief Justice to preside over the impeachment trial of a sitting President. But Donald Trump is not a sitting President, which means that the Chief Justice need not preside at his trial—just as the Chief Justice does not preside over impeachment trials of other officials. The Framers required the Chief Justice to preside over the trial of a sitting President to ensure that the Vice President, as President of the Senate, does not oversee a trial where conviction would result in her ascending to the presidency. That concern is not implicated in a trial of a former President.

Finally, President Trump wrongly suggests that, because he is now a private citizen, convicting and disqualifying him would raise concerns under the Bill of Attainder Clause, which prohibits Congress from following the old English practice of passing laws that single out a specific individual for punishment.[46] But unlike in the Supreme Court cases cited by President Trump,[47] which involved legislative attempts to punish individuals for their private conduct, President Trump was impeached by the House while he was in office for abuses he committed as a sitting President. He does not even try to claim that the House lacked authority to impeach him for those abuses.

[45] Opp. at 23; U.S. Const., Art. I, § 3, cl. 6.
[46] *See* Opp. at 15-17; *see also* U.S. Const., Art. I, § 9, cl. 3.
[47] Opp. at 16-17.

Trying, convicting, and disqualifying him in the Senate based on those same abuses poses no risk of subjecting a private party to punitive legislative action targeting his private conduct.

History: The "originalist" case for the Senate's jurisdiction here could hardly be stronger. President Trump does not dispute that the Framers looked to English practice as a model for the federal impeachment power. And President Trump concedes that, in the English system, officials could be impeached and disqualified after leaving office.[48] In fact, as we described in our opening brief (at 51), Warren Hastings, a former official, faced impeachment charges in England even as the Framers gathered in Philadelphia to draft our Constitution—and the Framers cited his case as one in which impeachment was appropriate. President Trump is therefore left to make the implausible argument that the Framers intended to depart from this settled English practice without saying so.

President Trump similarly concedes that numerous state constitutions during the founding era provided for the impeachment of former officials.[49] None prohibited such impeachments. Indeed, in some states, *only* former officials could be impeached, which confirms that the Framers surely understood that the impeachment power could also encompass former officials. Had they intended to depart from that understanding, they would have said so.

Precedent dating back more than 200 years makes the Senate's jurisdiction here even clearer—as noted by, among many others, Professor Steven Calabresi, Co-Chairman of the Federalist Society's Board of Directors.[50] After leaving office, President John Quincy Adams recognized that he was "amenable to impeachment by [the] House for everything I did during the

---

[48] Opp. at 20.

[49] Opp. at 21.

[50] Steven G. Calabresi and Norman Eisen, *We Disagree on a Lot. But We Both Think Trump Should Be Convicted*, N.Y. Times (Jan. 13, 2021).

time I held any public office."[51] And the Senate has several times affirmed that it has the power to try, convict, and disqualify officials after they leave office. When Senator Blount was expelled from the Senate after being impeached in 1798, he expressly disavowed at his Senate trial the radical claim (made here by President Trump) that former officials were categorically exempt from trial.[52]

When Secretary of War Belknap was impeached in 1876 shortly after resigning, the Senate squarely rejected his argument that there was no jurisdiction to try him as a former official.[53] President Trump asserts that the Senate's exercise of jurisdiction in the Belknap trial should not be treated as precedent because Belknap was ultimately acquitted. But before Belknap was acquitted, the Senate rejected the exact same jurisdictional claim that President Trump presses here.[54] President Trump relies at length on Joseph Story to support that now-rejected claim.[55] But Story's conclusions were equivocal—indeed, he recognized that impeachment of former officers could still serve a purpose because "a judgment of disqualification might still be pronounced."[56]

If there were any doubt on the question, when the House impeached Judge Archbald in 1912, based in part on his conduct in a prior judgeship, "a majority of the [S]enators voting saw no

---

[51] Cong. Globe, 29th Cong., 1st Sess. 641 (1846).

[52] Eleanore Bushnell, *Crimes, Follies, and Misfortunes: The Federal Impeachment Trials*, at 30 (1992).

[53] Brian C. Kalt, *The Constitutional Case for the Impeachability of Former Federal Officials: An Analysis of the Law, History, and Practice of Late Impeachment*, 6 Tex. Rev. L. & Pol. 13, 96 (2001).

[54] Opp. at 25-26. President Trump also points to opinions by Nebraska and Florida courts regarding their states' impeachment power. *See* Opp. at 28-30. But the Nebraska case involved an officer who had left office before the impeachment investigation even began, and the court found under state law that while a former officer could not be impeached and tried, a former officer could be tried if he had been in office at the time of his impeachment. *See State v. Hill*, 55 N.W. 794, 795, 798 (Neb. 1893); *see also* Opp. 34 n.86. In any event, the opinions of *state* courts interpreting *state* law in cases decided a century or two after the federal Constitution was drafted are not persuasive evidence of the scope of the federal impeachment power.

[55] Opp. at 31-32.

[56] Joseph Story, *Commentaries on the Constitution of the United States* § 801 (R. Rotunda & J. Nowak eds., 1987); *see also* Brian C. Kalt, *The Constitutional Case for the Impeachability of Former Federal Officials: An Analysis of the Law, History, and Practice of Late Impeachment*, 6 Tex. Rev. L. & Pol. 13, 123 (2001).

problem" with impeaching him for misconduct in his former office.[57] In more than 200 years, the Senate has *never* accepted the self-defeating argument that it lacks the power to try the impeachment of a former official. The Senate should not do so for the first time now.

Purpose of Impeachment: Once again failing to engage with the Constitution's plain text, President Trump argues that "[t]he purpose of impeachment is to remove someone from office."[58] But removal is not the only purpose of impeachment. In crafting the impeachment power, the Framers included two separate remedies—removal from office *as well as* disqualification from future officeholding. Distinct from the removal power, the disqualification power was intended to ensure that officials who abused their power were never again permitted to attain office from which they could threaten the American people. This animating purpose of disqualification—to protect the Nation from the return of a dangerous official—applies just as forcefully when the official has left office by the time the Senate tries his impeachment. President Trump does not even attempt to explain why the Framers would have provided that a *sitting* President found to have endangered the Nation should be disqualified from returning to office, but a *former* President found to have done the exact same thing should be free to return.

Nor can President Trump defend the perverse consequences that would result from his theory. The Framers feared more than anything a President who spared "no efforts or means whatever to get himself re-elected."[59] Thus, they understood that the paradigm case for impeachment would arise from a President's efforts to overturn an election. But elections, by

---

[57] *Id.* at 104.
[58] Opp. at 18.
[59] 2 The Records of the Federal Convention of 1787, at 64 (Max Farrand, ed., 1911).

definition, occur at the end of a President's term. It is inconceivable that the Framers designed impeachment to be virtually useless in a President's final weeks or days, when opportunities to interfere with the peaceful transfer of power are most present. And it is equally inconceivable that the Framers intended to create a remedy that would make no sense: disqualify a President from future office if he tried and succeeded to overturn an election, thus remaining in office, but not if—like President Trump—he tried and failed.

The consequences of President Trump's jurisdictional argument get more dangerous still. President Trump does not dispute that, if his theory were correct, the Senate would be powerless to address abuse by officials that comes to light only after they leave office. Nor does President Trump dispute that, under his theory, a President "who betrayed the public trust and was impeached could avoid accountability simply by resigning one minute before the Senate's final conviction vote."[60] The President could thus evade the Senate's disqualification power by resigning, then could later return to office, where he would be free to betray the public trust all over again. This loophole would "practically annihilate the power of impeachment in all cases of guilt clearly provable."[61]

President Trump points out that Congress in the past has declined to impeach, convict, and disqualify officials after they leave office. President Trump asks why, for example, the House did not impeach President Nixon after he resigned.[62] The answer is that impeachment, conviction, and disqualification were unnecessary where President Nixon resigned in disgrace, acknowledged wrongdoing, and was already barred from running again for President by the Twenty-Second

---

[60] *Constitutional Law Scholars on Impeaching Former Officers* at 2 (Jan. 21, 2021).
[61] 4 Cong. Rec. at 79 (1876) (Opinion of Senator Thurman).
[62] Opp. at 27.

Amendment.[63] By contrast, President Trump has described his conduct as "totally appropriate,"[64] refused to accept responsibility for his abuses, and is eligible to seek the Presidency—and assault the democratic process—yet again.

That Congress has previously found it unnecessary to disqualify former officials despite its clear power to do so demonstrates that Congress does not take this step lightly. It also demonstrates that there is no merit to President Trump's spurious claim that disqualifying him here would open the floodgates and allow Congress to use impeachments to pursue old grudges or settle old scores—particularly given that President Trump was still in office when he was impeached.[65] And, above all else, it highlights the unprecedented danger created by President Trump's effort to cling to power by inciting an attack on Congress. The Senate must reject President Trump's invitation to eviscerate one of the Senate's most important tools for protecting the Nation against officials who attempt to subvert our democracy.

C. The First Amendment Provides No Defense to Conviction and Disqualification

President Trump's reliance on the First Amendment is an insult to the values that the First Amendment enshrines. In the words of nearly 150 First Amendment lawyers and constitutional scholars, President Trump's First Amendment defense is "legally frivolous."[66]

---

[63] *See* President Nixon's Resignation Speech, August 8, 1974; *see also* U.S. Const. amend. XXII ("No person shall be elected to the office of the President more than twice …").

[64] Kevin Liptak & Betsy Klein, *Defiant Trump Denounces Violence but Takes No Responsibility for Inciting Deadly Riot*, CNN (Jan. 12, 2021).

[65] Opp. at 35.

[66] *Constitutional Law Scholars on President Trump's First Amendment Defense* at 1-2 (Feb. 5, 2021); *see also* Nicholas Fandos et al., *144 Constitutional Lawyers Call Trump's First Amendment Defense 'Legally Frivolous,'* N.Y. Times (Feb. 5, 2021).

President Trump argues that he is "protected by the First Amendment" "[l]ike all Americans."[67] He is wrong from the beginning: the President is not "[l]ike all Americans." The First Amendment has no application in an impeachment proceeding, which does not seek to punish unlawful speech, but instead to protect the Nation from a President who violated his oath of office and abused the public trust.

Under President Trump's view of the First Amendment, even a sitting President who strenuously urged States to secede from the Union and rebel against the federal government would be immune from impeachment. Likewise, a President could declare his loyalty to a foreign power or publicly renounce his oath "to preserve, protect, and defend the Constitution"—all without fear of impeachment.[68] The First Amendment provides no such immunity for a President who has committed "high Crimes and Misdemeanors."

In fact, the Senate has confirmed that the First Amendment does not limit its power to convict in an impeachment proceeding. In 1804, the Senate convicted Judge John Pickering in part for inflammatory and politically charged statements he made from the bench.[69] No precedent supports President Trump's contrary view. He cites the impeachment of President Johnson in 1868, contending that the Senate there established that a President cannot be convicted and disqualified

---

[67] Answer at 4-5, 10; Opp. at 37-66.

[68] *See Constitutional Law Scholars on President Trump's First Amendment Defense* at 1; *see also* Peter D. Keisler & Richard D. Bernstein, *Freedom of Speech Doesn't Mean What Trump's Lawyers Want It to Mean*, The Atlantic (Feb. 2021) (arguing that President Trump's First Amendment argument is wrong and could produce the absurd result that a President could not be impeached if he or she "burned an American flag on national television to demonstrate contempt for the country he or she had been chosen to lead" or "wore a swastika while leading a Nazi march through a Jewish neighborhood").

[69] Keith E. Whittington, *Is There a Free Speech Defense to an Impeachment?*, Lawfare (Jan. 19, 2021).

based on his speech.[70] But the Senate set no such precedent in President Johnson's impeachment. As President Trump notes, one of the articles of impeachment charged President Johnson with insulting and denouncing Congress by "mak[ing] and declar[ing] … certain intemperate, inflammatory, and scandalous harangues … [which] are peculiarly indecent and unbecoming in the Chief Magistrate of the United States."[71] While some Senators expressed concern that President Johnson's remarks were constitutionally protected,[72] others disagreed. Senator Jacob Howard, for example, stated that "[n]o question of the 'freedom of speech' arises here."[73] Ultimately the Senate never voted on the article and thus made no judgment about the relevance of the First Amendment. In any event, there is no comparison between President Johnson's "intemperate" broadsides and President Trump's incitement of an insurrection.

Indeed, even if—contrary to precedent and scholarship—the First Amendment were understood to restrict Congress's power over impeachments, it still would not protect President Trump's calls to violence.[74] In *Brandenburg v. Ohio*, the Supreme Court explained that, while the First Amendment prohibits states from punishing "mere advocacy," it does *not* preclude punishment for speech that is "is directed to inciting or producing imminent lawless action and is likely to incite or produce such action."[75] President Trump's speech falls squarely within this exception for incitement. His statements on January 6, particularly in the context of his prior remarks, were

---

[70] Opp. at 65-66.
[71] *The Impeachment of Andrew Johnson (1868) President of the United States*, U.S. Senate, www.senate.gov/artandhistory/history/common/briefing/Impeachment_Johnson.htm#7.
[72] 3 Trial of Andrew Johnson 206 (1868) (speech of Sen. Joseph Fowler).
[73] *Id.* at 49 (speech of Sen. Jacob Howard).
[74] *Brandenburg v. Ohio*, 395 U.S. 444, 449 (1969).
[75] *Id.* at 447.

"directed to" and "likely to incite or produce" imminent unlawful action.[76] President Trump incited a crowd to go to the Capitol and fight, immediately before they stormed the Capitol.

These statements would not be protected whether they were made by an elected official, a civil servant, or a private citizen—contrary to President Trump's lengthy argument that those distinctions should matter.[77] President Trump is not helped by his reliance on a case concerning punishment for statements made by an elected official "as a private citizen" that "did not present a danger to the administration of justice."[78] Nor does the Supreme Court's recognition that an elected legislator could not be excluded from state office for "criticizing public policy" advance President Trump's claim, where the Court distinguished that situation from one in which "a legislator swears to an oath pro forma while … manifesting his … indifference to the oath."[79] President Trump's speech was not a criticism of public policy—rather, it was a repudiation of his oath of office as he incited a violent insurrection and then manifested callous indifference to its deadly consequences.

President Trump attempts to equate his January 6 speech to statements by other politicians, arguing that convicting him will chill political speech.[80] But context matters under the First Amendment. While other political figures have used heated rhetoric, none of the speeches that President Trump cites bears any resemblance to President Trump's anti-democratic effort to prolong his presidency by exhorting a mob to attack the Congress. President Trump spoke to

[76] *Constitutional Law Scholars on President Trump's First Amendment Defense* at 2-3 (concluding that President Trump's "words and conduct were not protected" under the First Amendment because they were "in the words of the *Brandenburg* case, 'directed to inciting or producing imminent lawless action and … likely to … produce such action'").

[77] Opp. at 41-46 (citing *Wood v. Georgia*, 370 U.S. 375 (1962), and *Bond v. Floyd*, 385 U.S. 116 (1966)).

[78] *See Wood*, 370 U.S. at 382, 393, 395.

[79] *Bond*, 385 U.S. at 132, 136.

[80] Opp. at 63-64.

supporters who were angry, prepared for violence, and intent on disrupting Congress's counting of the electoral votes. Knowing all that, he launched into an inflammatory speech that was bound to result in the violence that followed. And, of great significance, as his supporters overtook the Capitol, instead of acting to stop them, he watched delightedly on television, continued to disparage his Vice President, and lobbied Senators to overturn the election. That conduct is impeachable.

D. President Trump Has Received From Congress All The Process He Was Due

President Trump's claim that the House denied him due process by moving too quickly to impeach him has no grounding in law or fact. It also misunderstands the constitutional process for impeachments: his impeachment *trial* occurs in the Senate, not in the House.

The Constitution vests the House with the "sole Power of Impeachment"[81] and the power to "determine the Rules of its Proceedings."[82] Here, the House had to move quickly to address President Trump's dangerous misconduct, to discourage him from engaging in further abuse during the last days of his term, and to send an immediate signal that such an attack on our core democratic institutions will not be tolerated. And it was appropriate for the House to impeach without a lengthy investigation because the most relevant evidence against him is a matter of undisputed public record—the underlying events played out on live television and social media and were witnessed firsthand by Members of Congress.

President Trump ignores reality in arguing that there was no exigency that justified the House's urgent impeachment of him.[83] His actions after January 6 established that he posed a

---

[81] U.S. Const., Art. I, § 2, cl. 5.
[82] U.S. Const., Art. I, § 5, cl. 2.
[83] Opp. at 68-71.

continuing, immediate threat to our democracy. When the House impeached him one week after the insurrection, it was rightly concerned that "a President capable of fomenting a violent insurrection in the Capitol is capable of greater dangers still."[84] Importantly, President Trump had failed to show any remorse for the violence and instead continued to fan the flames.[85]

In light of this ongoing threat, five days after the assault on the Capitol, an article of impeachment was introduced in the House and referred to the House Committee on the Judiciary. During a hearing the following day, the Chairman of the Judiciary Committee submitted a 50-page report documenting the Committee's findings supporting impeachment, relying heavily on recorded speeches and actions.[86] One day later—on January 13, 2021—the House voted to impeach President Trump with bipartisan support on charges that he incited an insurrection. The article of impeachment was adopted with the support of 232 House Members, including every Democrat and ten Republicans.[87] This House impeachment provided President Trump with all the process he was due.

President Trump now argues that the House did not need to act expeditiously because his term ended without "apocalyptic predictions … coming to pass."[88] That ignores the fact that the impeachment itself limited the danger posed by President Trump. The House sent a clear message

---

[84] *House Judiciary Committee Majority Staff Report: Materials in Support of H. Res. 24, Impeaching Donald John Trump, President of the United States, for High Crimes and Misdemeanors*, at 3, 117th Cong (Jan. 12, 2021).

[85] *See id.* at 40-43.

[86] *House Judiciary Committee Majority Staff Report: Materials in Support of H. Res. 24, Impeaching Donald John Trump, President of the United States, for High Crimes and Misdemeanors*, 117th Cong (Jan. 12, 2021).

[87] Clerk of the U.S. House of Representatives, Roll Call 17, H. Res. 24 (Jan. 13, 2021).

[88] Opp. at 69.

that the President's conduct would not be tolerated, and President Trump was undoubtedly chastened in the final days of his term, knowing that he would face a Senate impeachment trial.

For these reasons, there was no procedural flaw in the House's impeachment of President Trump. But even if there were, that would be irrelevant to the Senate's separate exercise of its "sole Power *to try* all Impeachments."[89] Any defect in the House's impeachment proceedings—which are not an impeachment trial—could be cured when the evidence is presented to the Senate at trial.

President Trump incorrectly suggests that the Senate is like an appellate court, reviewing the decision of a lower court.[90] But that is not how the Framers structured the impeachment power: the House has the sole power to impeach, and the Senate has the sole power to try the impeachment and convict. It is the constitutional duty of *the Senate* to consider the evidence and decide for itself whether President Trump is guilty of inciting an insurrection. And President Trump has been provided with every opportunity to defend himself in his Senate trial, including additional time to prepare, extensive pretrial briefing,[91] and the opportunity to testify, which he declined.[92]

President Trump mistakenly points to the timing of the Senate impeachment trial to insist that there was no exigency in the House's impeachment. But the timing of the Senate trial was negotiated by leaders from both parties. Indeed, "Senate Republicans had requested *more time* to

[89] U.S. Const., Art. I, § 3, cl. 6 (emphasis added).
[90] Opp. at 70.
[91] S. Res. 16, 117th Cong. (2021).
[92] *See* Ltr. from Representative Raskin to President Trump (Feb. 4, 2021) (inviting President Trump to provide testimony); Ltr. from Bruce Castor to Representative Raskin (Feb. 4, 2021) (declining invitation).

allow Trump's lawyers to prepare."[93] The Senate then passed a resolution providing that the trial would begin on February 9, 2021.[94]

Finally, the allegation that Senator Leahy will be biased in presiding over the impeachment trial is both offensive and mistaken.[95] As Senator Leahy has explained: "I consider holding the office of the president pro tempore and the responsibilities that come with it to be one of the highest honors and most serious responsibilities of my career. When I preside over the impeachment trial of former President Donald Trump, I will not waver from my constitutional and sworn obligations to administer the trial with fairness, in accordance with the Constitution and the laws."[96]

E. The Senate Is Not Limited To The Standards Of Criminal Law

President Trump mistakenly contends that conviction by the Senate is only permitted where the House charges a violation of criminal law.[97] Under President Trump's view of the Senate's power to try impeachments, even if every Senator found that all of the allegations in the article were true, the Senate could not convict because the article does not specifically "describe any violation of law."[98] As Chuck Cooper recently put it, the argument that the alleged conduct does not rise to the level of an impeachable offense is "a hard argument to make with a straight face."[99] And as Steven

---

[93] Dartunorro Clark, *House Managers Deliver Impeachment Article Against Trump, Kicking Off Trial Preparations*, NBC News (Jan. 25, 2021) (emphasis added); Mike DeBonis, *Senate Ends Standoff, Agrees to Start Trump's Impeachment Trial Feb. 9*, Wash. Post (Jan. 22, 2021).

[94] S. Res. 16, 117th Cong. (2021).

[95] *See* Opp. at 70.

[96] Senator Patrick Leahy, Comment on Presiding Over the Impeachment Trial of President Donald Trump (Jan. 25, 2021).

[97] Opp. at 26, 72-74.

[98] Opp. at 73.

[99] Chuck Cooper, *The Constitution Doesn't Bar Trump's Impeachment Trial*, Wall Street Journal (Feb. 7, 2021).

Calabresi explained, "Whether or not Trump's words were a violation of the criminal law, they fall squarely within the Framers' definition of 'a High Crime and Misdemeanor.'"[100] Although President Trump's conduct may separately violate the criminal code, impeachment is not limited to criminal offenses, nor is it governed by the standards of proof that may apply in a criminal trial.[101] Indeed, even the legal scholar on whom President Trump relies has previously acknowledged that impeachment has never been understood to require criminal conduct.[102] The House therefore was not required to charge—and the Senate need not find—that President Trump committed any criminal offense.

Impeachment was conceived in the English Parliament as a method to control the King's ministers. It was not limited to accusations of criminal wrongdoing, but instead included broader, non-criminal offenses including abuse of power, corruption, and neglect of duty.[103] The Framers were aware of this history and understood that impeachment and conviction must reach a broad array of conduct beyond criminal misconduct, including abuse of power, betrayal of the Nation, and

---

[100] Steve Calabresi, *Trump Should Be Convicted By The Senate*, Daily Caller (Jan. 28, 2021).

[101] *See* H. Rep. No. 116-346 at 56-62.

[102] *See* Jonathan Turley, Written Statement, *The Impeachment Inquiry into President Donald J. Trump: The "Constitutional Basis" for Presidential Impeachment*, at 10-11 (Dec. 4, 2019) (acknowledging that, since the Founding, it has been understood that impeachable acts need not constitute criminal offenses); *see also Constitutional Law Scholars on President Trump's First Amendment Defense* at 1 (Feb. 5, 2021) (explaining that "Congress's power to impeach is not limited to *unlawful* acts" and that "violations of an officer's oath of office can constitute impeachable 'high Crimes or misdemeanors' under the Constitution even if no law has been violated"); Alan Dershowitz, *The Case Against Impeaching Trump*, at 26-27 (2018) (conceding that, if it were true that impeachment were warranted only for criminal law violations, it would lead to the absurd results that the President could not be impeached even if he allowed an enemy power to invade and conquer American territory). President Trump also mistakenly cites Professor Paul Campos, apparently to support his argument about what conduct is impeachable. Opp. at 66 n.195. But Professor Campos's article addressed a different subject—the standard for removing a sitting President under the Twenty-Fifth Amendment—and, in any event, he has since confirmed that it does not stand for the proposition for which President Trump cites it. Paul Campos, *That was a right pretty speech, sir. But I ask you, what is a contract?*, Lawyers, Guns & Money (Feb. 8, 2021).

[103] H. Rep. No. 116-346 at 57 (citing 2 J. Story, *Commentaries on the Constitution of the United States*, 268 (1833)).

corruption of the office and of elections.[104] As Alexander Hamilton explained in the *Federalist Papers*, impeachable offenses are defined by "the abuse or violation of some public trust"; they "are of a nature which may with peculiar propriety be denominated POLITICAL, as they relate chiefly to injuries done immediately to the society itself."[105] For these reasons, a "'requirement of criminality would be incompatible with the intent of the [F]ramers to provide a mechanism broad enough to maintain the integrity of constitutional government.'"[106]

History and precedent confirm that conduct need not be criminal to be impeachable. Judge Archbald, for instance, was removed in 1912 for non-criminal speculation in coal properties, and Judge Ritter was removed in 1936 for the non-criminal act of bringing his court into scandal and disrepute.[107] Likewise, the House Judiciary Committee's allegations against President Nixon contained claims encompassing non-criminal acts, although President Nixon resigned before the House itself could consider impeachment.[108] In accord with that precedent, the Senate has also

---

[104] *Id.* (citing Peter Charles Hoffer & N. E. H. Hull, *Impeachment in America, 1635–1805*, at 1-95 (1984), and Frank O. Bowman, III, *High Crimes and Misdemeanors: A History of Impeachment for the Age of Trump*, at 244 (2019)).

[105] Alexander Hamilton, Federalist No. 65; *see also* Joseph Story, *Commentaries on the Constitution of the United States* § 801 (R. Rotunda & J. Nowak eds., 1987) (explaining that impeachment is a political, not a criminal proceeding, intended "not … to punish an offender" by threatening deprivation of his life or liberty, but rather to "secure the state" by "divest[ing] him of his political capacity"); H. Rep. No. 116-346 at 62.

[106] Staff of H. Comm. on the Judiciary, *Constitutional Grounds for Presidential Impeachment 93d Cong.*, at 25 (Comm. Print 1974).

[107] H. Rep. No. 116-346 at 58 (citing *Report of the Committee on the Judiciary, Robert W. Archbald, Judge of the United States Commerce Court*, H. Rep. No. 62–946 (1912), and H. Res. 422, 74th Cong. (1936)).

[108] *Id.* (citing *Committee Report on Nixon Articles of Impeachment* (1974)).

consistently rejected suggestions that it adopt a standard of proof borrowed from the criminal law, choosing instead to allow each Senator to determine how best to judge the facts presented.[109]

While President Trump's efforts to overturn the results of the 2020 election, culminating in his incitement of the January 6 insurrection, very well may have violated the criminal law, that is beside the point here. The only question before the Senate is whether President Trump's violation of his oath and breach of the public trust warrant conviction and disqualification from future officeholding. Here, there is no doubt that it does. Indeed, it is difficult to imagine conduct more deserving of conviction and disqualification than that for which President Trump was impeached.

F. The Article Does Not Charge Multiple Instances Of Impeachable Conduct

President Trump finally errs in arguing that the article of impeachment impermissibly charges "multiple alleged wrongs" and that, as a result, it would be "impossible" for a conviction to comply with the Constitutional requirement that it rest on a two-thirds vote of the Senators present.[110] This argument misconstrues the text of the article and the relevant precedent.

The article does not, as President Trump claims, charge multiple impeachable offenses. Rather, it charges that President Trump engaged in a single course of impeachable conduct in inciting an insurrection on January 6. While the article explains that President Trump employed

---

[109] *See, e.g.*, 132 Cong. Rec. S15489-S15490 (daily ed. Oct. 7, 1986) (in his 1986 impeachment proceedings, Judge Harry E. Claiborne moved to designate "beyond a reasonable doubt" as the standard of proof for his conviction; the Senate rejected that request, and one of the House managers explained that the Senate had historically allowed each Member to exercise his or her own personal judgment in impeachment cases); *Report of the Senate Impeachment Trial Committee on the Articles Against Judge Alcee Hastings: Hearings before the Senate Impeachment Trial Committee* (Part 1) 101st Cong., 1st Sess. 73-75 (when a question arose about the appropriate standard of proof during the 1989 impeachment of Judge Alcee Hastings, a Senator explained that there was no set standard; rather "[i]t is what is in the mind of every Senator.... it is what everybody decides for themselves").

[110] Opp. at 71-72; *see also* U.S. Const., Art. I § 3, cl. 6 (conviction requires "the Concurrence of two thirds of the Members present"); Rule XXIII, *Rules of Procedure and Practice in the Senate When Sitting on Impeachment Trials* (rev. Aug. 16, 1986) (providing that articles of impeachment may not be "divisible for the purpose of voting thereon").

various tactics, over the course of months, "to subvert and obstruct the certification of the results of the 2020 Presidential election," it also makes clear that these activities merely provided the kindling, which President Trump set aflame when he incited insurrection on January 6.[111] Of course, this prior course of conduct is also relevant in illuminating President Trump's state of mind on January 6 when he exhorted his followers to march to the Capitol and "fight like hell."

President Trump appears to borrow his argument from a similar one made (unsuccessfully) during the impeachment trial of President Clinton.[112] But any comparison to President Clinton's impeachment does not help President Trump here. The articles in President Clinton's impeachment charged that he engaged in "one or more" improper acts.[113] Thus, unlike this article, the Senate could have convicted President Clinton without a two-thirds agreement on which of the charged improper acts he committed. Even so, the Senate *rejected* President Clinton's effort to dismiss the articles on the ground that they charged multiple offenses.[114] As the House Managers explained, the Senate's Rules (which remain in effect today) "specifically contemplate that the House may draft articles of impeachment" containing multiple specifications, "and prior rulings of the Senate have

---

[111] H. Res. 24, 117th Cong. (2021).

[112] Opp. at 71 (quoting the 2020 Trial Memorandum of President Donald J. Trump (at 107-108), which in turn invoked the "duplicity" argument made during the Clinton impeachment trial).

[113] H. Res. 611, 105th Cong. (1998).

[114] 145 Cong. Rec. S961, S973-S974 (daily ed. Jan. 25, 1999).

held that such drafting is not deficient."[115] If President Clinton's claim failed—where the articles in fact alleged multiple, distinct acts of impeachable conduct—then so too must President Trump's.

* * *

[115] *Reply of United States House of Representatives to Trial Memorandum of President William Jefferson Clinton* (Jan. 14, 1999) [145 Cong. Rec. S215-21 (daily ed. Jan. 14, 1999)] at 25 (*reprinted in Proceedings of the United States Senate in the Impeachment Trial of President William Jefferson Clinton*, S. Doc. 106-4, 106th Cong., 1st Sess. (Feb. 12, 1999)); *see also Amending the Rules of Procedure and Practice in the Senate When Sitting on Impeachment Trials,* Report of the Comm. on Rules and Administration, S. Rep. No. 99-401, 99th Cong., 2nd Sess., at 8 (1986) (recognizing that "the most judicious and efficacious" approach to drafting articles of impeachment would be to present "broadly based charges" containing multiple enumerated specifications, and noting that the new rules would allow for conviction where a Senator found the accused guilty "of one or more of the enumerated specifications").